Dawn on our Darkness

A Nativity Play

Richard Tydeman

SAMUEL FRENCH

FOUNDED 1830

SAMUELFRENCH-LONDON.CO.UK
SAMUELFRENCH.COM

DAWN ON OUR DARKNESS

This play is designed for performance in any Church or Hall.

A reasonably central acting area is required for scenes with JOSEPH *and* MARY. *Well away from the centre, and widely separated from each other, are the three positions occupied respectively by* HEROD, DAN *and* CASPAR. *Ideally, each of these is illuminated by an independently controlled spot-light; if this is not practicable, then* HEROD, DAN *and* CASPAR *will have to move into the central lighted area to speak their lines and then retire into the shadows again. In addition, there should be a spot-light focused on the altar, or on a cross at the back of the stage. The action is continuous and there are no curtains.*

The CHORUS, *consisting of not less than two and not more than ten people, enter and arrange themselves in groups at the sides. Any lighting of the* CHORUS *is at the discretion of the Producer who will also decide which lines the* CHORUS *will speak all together, and which shall be spoken by groups or individuals in order to achieve the best variation and contrast. The judicious use of music at the beginning and end, and between the different scenes, is strongly recommended.*

The play begins in darkness.

CHORUS   Darkness upon the face of all the deep.
Heavy with sleep, the people sit in darkness.
As on the day that Moses stretched his hand,
That over Egypt's land their hearts should melt
In darkness that may be felt.
Gross darkness then shall cover all the earth;
The people walk in darkness without mirth;
In death's cold shadow even from their birth.
God said, Let there be light! And forth there shone
A radiance bright. The word was spoken;
The power of darkness broken.
In the beginning was the Word. Creation heard
And trembled into life. Let us make man,

Said God, in our own image. But the plan
Broke under human sin. And so began
This second reign of darkness upon the earth
Which man himself had dealt:
Darkness that may be felt.
(*Light on* HEROD.)

HEROD   Now, let's have no nonsense about this. There's nothing the matter with darkness as such. For instance, it's much easier to go to sleep in the dark. We all need a bit of a rest from the glare of the sun, you know. Observe a due proportion; learn to use darkness as an ally. When I was young I said to myself: Herod, I said, you will get nowhere unless you are prepared to compromise. Night is as good as day for any sort of activity, and sometimes a good deal better.
(*Light off* HEROD.)

CHORUS   This is the condemnation: that light is come
Into the world, and men preferred the darkness
Because their deeds were evil.
(*Light on* DAN *the Shepherd.*)

DAN   Don't be too hard on us, if you please. We shepherds have to spend a lot of time in darkness. There's queer things go on at night, and wild animals to watch for, and thieves and robbers will even break into a sheepfold. We don't like the darkness, mind you; there's times when we can be sore afraid in it, but we mostly get used to it in time, just as we get used to Roman soldiers, and tax collectors, and shortage of water. There's nothing you can do about such things. Of course, when the Messiah comes—but men have been saying that for centuries. We go on saying it, but we don't really believe it any more.
(*Light off* DAN.)

CHORUS   There is no darkness deeper than the shade
Man's disbelief has made.
This is the greatest darkness, the despair
Of those who cease to care.
(*Light on* CASPAR.)

CASPAR   I do assure you that this is not true of all of us. Day after day I wait eagerly for the darkness to come again;

for only in the darkness can one see the stars. To me, the beauties of the day are as nothing compared with the wonders of the night: the great moon sailing serenely among the clouds, not shining fiercely as the sun does, so that one may not look upon him steadily and live; the moon shines gently. And the stars! The great Orion, and that mystic Plough turning its endless furrow around the North Star. Planets, the wanderers that come and go, and sometimes a comet trailing streams of glory. Oh, never despair in darkness, my friends, for there is always new hope shining for those who look up.

(*Light off* CASPAR.)

CHORUS There shall be signs
In the sun and in the moon and in the stars;
Upon the earth, distress, perplexity,
And men's hearts failing them for fear.
And when these things begin to come to pass,
Then look up, and lift your heads on high.
Redemption draweth nigh.

(*Light on* MARY, *kneeling, in central area.*)

VOICE OF GABRIEL (*which could be one of the* CHORUS)
I, Gabriel, that in God's presence stand,
Am sent into this land
For now is man's salvation near at hand.
In Nazareth I seek
A maiden meek,
And to that maiden Mary will I speak.

(MARY *looks up, surprised.*)
Hail, highly favoured, bless'd of womankind,
The Lord is with thee.

MARY Good sir, I find
This salutation strange unto my mind.

GABRIEL Fear not. For in God's favour very great
Shall be thy state.
All men shall celebrate
The holy child conceived within thy womb
Who shall by doom
Bring light and life from darkness and the tomb.

MARY How this shall be I know not. Yet I bow
My head in wonder now,

And my obedience I humbly vow.

(*Light off* MARY.)

CHORUS   The ways of God
Are most distinctly odd.
The wit of man
Could have devised a plan
A deal less droll
Than all this rigmarole.
What man of sense
Would go to such expense
His trust implying,
And slenderly relying
Upon one maiden's word?
How absurd!

(*Light on* HEROD.)

HEROD   Now, that's the first sensible thing we've heard so far. Why, and I ask you again, why in the name of all that's logical, why should the Almighty need to go to such lengths and take such risks when he could have come to me? Have I not built up a truly magnificent kingdom? Have I not brought about the perfect compromise between Church and State? On the one hand I have made peace with the Romans and encouraged western civilisation; on the other hand I have rebuilt the Temple so gloriously that even Solomon would be lost in admiration if he could see it.

Here is the perfect setting for the Messiah to be born; here is a palace, comfort, riches, food, drink, servants, and perhaps most important of all, here is security. A Messiah born into my family could be guaranteed the sort of upbringing he deserved. Everything I have is at the disposal of the Almighty. All he had to do was to ask me.

Instead of that, what happens? My wife turns against me and I have to destroy her. My children turn against me and I have to destroy them. I spend the whole of my life doing what I can for other people, and not a soul does anything for me.

Well, let the Almighty beware what messages he sends to simple village women; and let the babies of village

women beware too. I can destroy them any time I like.
Do you wonder I prefer darkness? At least a man can
be alone in darkness. The light brings too many people
out looking and spying and seeing things they have no
business to see. I hate the light.
(*Light off* HEROD.)

CHORUS　　This is the condemnation: that light is come
Into the world, and men preferred the darkness
Because their deeds were evil.
But now is the night far spent. Day is at hand.
The Sun of Righteousness, the Morning Star,
More brilliant far than all created light,
Dawns on our sight.
(*Light on central area.* JOSEPH *is measuring a piece of
wood.* MARY *enters carrying a letter.*)

MARY　Joseph, what's this word? (*He is pre-occupied.*) Joseph.

JOSEPH　Yes, my dear?

MARY　What's this word?

JOSEPH　(*seeing the letter*) Where did you get that?

MARY　You left it on the table. It says you have to go some-
where, but I can't read the name of the place.

JOSEPH　Bethlehem.

MARY　Bethlehem! But that's miles and miles away—the other
side of Jerusalem.

JOSEPH　I know.

MARY　Then why——?

JOSEPH　It's an order, by decree of Caesar Augustus himself.

MARY　Oh, the Romans. What do they want now?

JOSEPH　Principally, money. But they are taking the opportunity
to count us all as well, (*Sardonically.*) to make sure none
of us pay twice.

MARY　And so——?

JOSEPH　And so we all go back where we belong: the House of
David to the City of David—in other words, Joseph to
Bethlehem.

MARY　When?

JOSEPH　Next month.

MARY　Next month—but that's——

JOSEPH　I know.

MARY　It will be a long way to travel.

JOSEPH There's no need for you to come.

MARY Joseph! As if I'd let you go all that way without me.

JOSEPH In your condition——

MARY I won't hear another word. Why, supposing I stayed behind and my son were born here in Nazareth, then he wouldn't be officially counted with the House of David. (JOSEPH *tries to speak*.)

No, don't try and put me off. I know just what we'll do: we will set off next week and go straight to Jerusalem, and we'll stay with Elisabeth and Zacharias in—what's the name of their village?

JOSEPH Ein Karem.

MARY Yes. Oh Joseph, won't that be lovely? And then Elisabeth will be with me, just as I was with her when her son was born.

JOSEPH But, Mary——

MARY John will be nearly six months old now, and I'm longing to see him. And then we can all go over to Bethlehem on the taxing day and have a picnic.

JOSEPH (*grimly*) This will be no picnic.

MARY Now it's all decided. Don't you see the hand of God in this, Joseph? It all fits in. It's all—what's the word?— predestined. I'll go and start packing at once. (*Exit* MARY, *singing gaily*.)

JOSEPH Predestined it may be—but I don't like it. (*Light off central area*.)

CHORUS
How many miles to Bethlehem?
More than a hundred and ten,
In the dust and the mud, and the peril
Of beasts, and the wildness of men.
No journey to take in the winter—
Except at great Caesar's behest;
For the rain churns the roads in December,
And even a donkey must rest.
So the progress is slower and slower.
Zacharias and Elisabeth wait;
But the travellers keep to the high road
For fear of arriving too late.
And Joseph was right: it's no picnic;
It's more than most women could stand.

> And grey lines the white face of Mary,
> For she knows that her time is at hand.
> (*Light on* DAN *and* ELI, *shepherds, who could now be in the central area if more convenient.*)

DAN Poor woman, that's what I say, poor woman.

ELI Oh; that's nothing. My wife has had six, and she always comes up smiling afterwards.

DAN Maybe; but has she ever had to travel a hundred miles in that condition?

ELI How far?

DAN I'll bet you it's every bit of a hundred miles from Nazareth, and that's where the man said they came from. She looked near to death.

ELI You're exaggerating.

DAN You didn't see her. I did. I was sitting just here when they came by. 'Is that Bethlehem?' asks the man. 'That it is,' says I. 'Thank God,' says he, 'thank God.'

ELI And what did his wife say?

DAN She said nothing at all. She just looked at me.

ELI How?

DAN How what?

ELI How did she look at you?

DAN Oh, sort of grateful—and pathetic—and strong—and tender——

ELI Well, I've never seen anyone look like all those things at one time.

DAN Neither have I. That's why I can't get her out of my mind.

ELI Go on then: so what did you do?

DAN I said, 'Do you know your way to the inn?' And the man said, 'I shall know it when I get there.'

ELI But you sent the boy along with them just in case.

DAN Well, he had to go anyway, to fetch our supper.

ELI You're soft, that's what's the matter with you. Just because a woman looks at you——

DAN Ah, but you didn't see that look.

ELI No, I didn't.

DAN I wish you had. I wish to God you had. You wouldn't speak like that if you had.

ELI All right, so the boy went with them to show them the way to the inn.

DAN Well, that was the idea. But just as they were going, I said, 'I hope you've booked your room.'

ELI And they hadn't?

DAN They hadn't. 'Then you won't stand a chance,' I said, 'you won't stand an earthly.'

ELI Nor a heavenly, neither.

DAN 'Don't you know,' I said, 'that the taxing takes place to-morrow, and every bed in the inn has been booked for months and months. They've been turning people away all day, and now every spare bedroom in the village is let as well. Bethlehem is overflowing,' I said.

ELI Bursting at the seams, more like.

DAN So, that's all there is. They went off towards the town, and the boy went with them—and it's about time he was back, for that was an hour ago.

ELI The sun's getting low.

DAN It'll soon be dark again. I heard a wolf last night.

ELI The jackals were howling too.

DAN Darkness is a terrible thing.

ELI Terrible.

BOY (off) Hulloo!

DAN There he is. There's the boy. (Calling.) We're over here. (To ELI.) Well, at least he hasn't brought them back. (The BOY enters.)
You're only just in time; the sun is setting.

BOY (out of breath) I ran all the way.

ELI Come on, tell us what happened?

BOY Where?

DAN The man and the woman; you took them to the inn?

BOY It was no use. There are people sleeping on the floor, in the barn, in the stables—everywhere.

DAN But when they saw the state the woman was in——?

BOY They pretended not to notice. They looked the other way. I think they just didn't want to know.

ELI Exactly what I said. That's typical, they didn't want to know.

DAN So?

BOY It looked pretty hopeless. We tried house after house. The man was getting desperate.

DAN And the woman?

BOY She just—looked.

DAN Ah.

ELI Well, go on. Where are they now?

BOY I had a brainwave. You remember that cave.

DAN What cave?

BOY Where we sheltered from a storm once. They kept cattle in it.

DAN I know—where a donkey tried to bite you.

BOY That's the one. I took them there.

ELI You took them to a cave?

BOY What else could I do? At least it's dry, and there's some straw, and sticks for a fire.

DAN But what about the animals?

BOY There was an old ox asleep in the corner, and one donkey —not the one that bit me. I think they'll be all right.

ELI (*shivering*) The sun's gone down.

DAN Too late to do anything else now. I reckon her child will be born tonight—in that cave—in the dark. Poor woman. Poor, poor woman.

(*Light off.*)

CHORUS   This is the darkest night of all the year.
In deepest fear the people sit in darkness;
Dwelling where sinful man has ever dwelt,
In darkness that may be felt.
Each for himself would grasp; heeding no cry
But passing by, they murmur in the darkness:
'The fate of those who have no place to go
We do not want to know.'

(*Light on* HEROD.)

HEROD Ah, night time again. Slaves, bring in lamps. That's better. Lamps are useful; they help you to see what you want to see, and then they can be put out. (*Looking off* L.) Why isn't the gate closed? Because of what? A beggar? Well, move him; drag him outside and close the gate at once. A beggar! (*Looking off* R.) How well the Temple looks by moonlight. Splendid building—better than Solomon's puny efforts. We could do with a little more gold leaf on the pinnacles perhaps; I'll see to that tomorrow. (*Looking off* L.) Don't argue with him, kick him! (*Clutching his stomach.*) I wish I knew why I get these pains in my stomach. I'm careful what I eat. Doctors these days don't seem to understand the human body at all. Too many lamps! The light is hurting my eyes. Take them away and leave me in the darkness.

(*Light off* HEROD. *Light on* CASPAR.)

CASPAR Hail gladdening light! Hail star of consolation. Melchior, Balthasar, the time has come.

(MELCHIOR *and* BALTHASAR *join him.*)

Yonder it shines—the King is born tonight.

MELCHIOR Everything is ready, Caspar. The camels are waiting. Have you taken the bearings?

CASPAR Due west, my brothers, over Judaea.

BALTHASAR Just the mountains of Moab between us. It shouldn't take long.

CASPAR Bring the gifts. Make sure we have not forgotten anything.

MELCHIOR I have heard that the King of Judaea has built a great new Temple. He must be a good man.

BALTHASAR It doesn't necessarily follow, but I hope you are right. From what I have heard, he seems old to have a baby son.

CASPAR The new king could be his grandson.

BALTHASAR Of course. We shall soon see. But we waste time talking; let us take the road.

MELCHIOR Lead on, bright star; we take the road.

CASPAR We take the road.

(*Light off. Light on* SHEPHERDS. DAN *is sitting up;* ELI *and* BOY *are asleep.*)

DAN I don't believe it.

ELI What's the matter now?

DAN Get your head out of that blanket and you'll see.

ELI (*emerging*) I don't know what you're talking about. I— why, it can't be daylight already, I've only just shut my eyes.

DAN And I haven't shut mine at all.

ELI Are you sure?

DAN Of course I'm sure. When it's my turn to watch, I keep my eyes open—not like some I could mention. The light came all of a sudden: one minute it was dark, and the next moment—whoosh! Just like that.

ELI Where's it coming from?

DAN I don't know. It's—— (*He points into the light.*) Look!

GABRIEL Be not afraid. I, Gabriel, am sent
With this intent
That I should bring you news most excellent.
For unto you in David's town, in joy
Is born a boy
Who with his light the darkness shall destroy.
This saviour who is Christ—be not afraid——
A gentle maid
Has wrapped with care and in a manger laid.

CHORUS Glory to God on high, this holy night,
Who on our darkness sheds eternal light.
Peace on the earth, true peace and great good will;
For God so loved mankind, and loves him still.

ELI Has it gone?

DAN The bright light has gone, but it still isn't as dark as it was before. Somehow I don't think it ever will be.

ELI What was it?

DAN The glory of the Lord.

ELI What's it mean?

DAN Well, it's important.

ELI Yes.

DAN And wonderful.

ELI Yes?

DAN And—and good.

ELI Yes, but what does it mean?

DAN I don't know.

ELI There was music, but I don't understand music.

DAN Ask the boy; he's musical.

ELI Would you believe it, he's still asleep! Hey, boy, wake up!

BOY What's that?

DAN Wake up, boy, strange things have been happening.

BOY I've had a marvellous dream.

ELI Never mind about your dreams——

BOY I dreamt that the King was born.

ELI (*scornfully*) He dreamt that the—now, wait a minute, that's what the voice said.

BOY What voice?

DAN While you were asleep we saw a—a vision.

ELI The saviour, the Christ, he said.

BOY Of course. Then we must go at once and see.

DAN Go where?

BOY Why, to the cave; where else?

ELI He's got that cave on the brain.

BOY But that's where they are, the maid and the baby.

DAN The voice said that too, and something about a manger.

BOY That's right. I told them they could use it as a cradle.

ELI *You* told them?

BOY It seemed a good idea. Did I do wrong?

DAN No, boy, you didn't do wrong. Come on, let's go and see.
(As they get up to go, the light is off.)

CHORUS Holly and snow, candles a-glow,
Tinsel and trimming of outward show.
Manger so bare, animals stare;
What's it to do with us? Why should we care?
Turkey and wine, tableware shine;
Come all ye faithful and sit down to dine.
Open the box, pass round the chocs;
Nobody's there but an ass and an ox.
Lonely the cave, cold as a grave;
Forgotten by those he came to save.
From manger cry, or cross on high:
Is it nothing to you, all ye that pass by?
(Light on HEROD.*)*

HEROD Doctors, did you say? Doctors from the east? Well, fetch them in, man; don't keep them waiting. None of the doctors here are any good; they don't understand my complaints at all.
(Enter CASPAR, MELCHIOR *and* BALTHASAR.*)*
Welcome gentlemen—er, my lords—er, your highnesses. We understand that you are doctors.

CASPAR Lord King?

HEROD You are doctors, are you not?

CASPAR Doctors, but not of medicine, sir.

HEROD Oh. Doctors of what, then?

CASPAR Of philosophy, of astronomy, of theology.

HEROD My steward is a fool. He gave me the wrong information.

CASPAR Allow me, lord King, to offer you a gift of gold.

HEROD Gold? What should I do with gold?

CASPAR Perhaps for the adornment of your Temple?

HEROD I need no help with that. I can afford all this myself. It is Herod's Temple; no one shall ever call it anything else.

MELCHIOR Permit me, then, to offer you this frankincense to burn upon your altar.

HEROD I have fifty thousand boxes full of incense, sir doctor. I burn it constantly, but the Almighty takes no notice. The pains in my stomach get worse, and no one cares.

BALTHASAR I happen to have with me an ointment of myrrh. Will you accept some?

HEROD Myrrh—for the stomach? In this country, myrrh is only used for anointing the dead. Oh, I see, you think I am dying, eh?

BALTHASAR By no means, O King.

HEROD Yes, you do; you have all come to witness my death, (*Shouting.*) haven't you?

CASPAR Not your death, sir, but perhaps your—retirement?

HEROD What do you mean by that?

CASPAR Now that the new King is born.

HEROD The new King?

MELCHIOR We have seen his star, in the east, and are come to worship him.

HEROD Wait there. (*Moving away.*) So that's the great secret, is it. The Almighty has been working behind my back again. They shall die! But no, I must be cunning; I must find out the truth first. What do the scribes say? "The King shall be born in Bethlehem". I'll send them there, and they can find him for me. (*Returning.*) Worthy doctors.

CASPAR My lord?

HEROD You will find the new-born King in Bethlehem. He is hidden from view. You will have to search diligently.

MELCHIOR Will you be pleased to come with us, sir?

HEROD I—er, I am not well. I shall hope to go later, when my health is restored. Meanwhile, be so good as to come back and tell me exactly where he is.

CASPAR Your wish is our command, lord King.

BALTHASAR We will convey your blessings, sir.

HEROD Do that. Go quickly.

    CASPAR We take the road at once.

    MELCHIOR We take the road.

    BALTHASAR With grateful thanks to you, we take the road.

    HEROD (*as they go*) Oh, and offer him those gifts you brought me. He will find them all useful—(*Aside.*) especially the myrrh. (*They have gone.*) Oh, my stomach!
(*Light off.*)

    CHORUS Once more the darkness lightens, and afar
Appears the star hung low upon the hills.
The faithful shepherd, self-appointed slave
And guardian to the child born in the cave,
Has found a room for Mary in his home.
The claims of Rome are satisfied with tax.
A little while the family relax,
And now the time has come to venture forth
And journey north.
(*Light on* MARY *holding Baby in her arms, with* DAN, ELI *and* BOY.)

    DAN I shall be truly sorry to see you go, you know.

    ELI Ah, so shall I.

    MARY You have been so kind.

    ELI Do you really have to go back?

    MARY We certainly do. Joseph has his work waiting for him in Nazareth, and goodness knows what the house will be like after all this time.

    BOY Mary, can I come with you?

    DAN What, just at lambing time? The idea!

    BOY You could manage without me.

    MARY It's a kind offer, but we couldn't take you, really. But one day, I promise, we'll come and see you again.

    BOY And you'll bring him too?

    MARY Of course, when he's a bit older.

    BOY I'll teach him how to be a shepherd, and how to know the sheep, and how to carry lambs, and——

    DAN And maybe he'll teach you a thing or two.

    BOY Such as what?

    DAN Such as how to keep your mouth shut. Look at him, the good little soul; he never makes a murmur.
(*Enter* JOSEPH.)

    JOSEPH Well, now everything is ready. We can start first thing in the morning. (*To* DAN.) My dear good friend, I don't know how to thank you enough.

DAN Don't thank me; it's the least we could do.

BOY I wish I could go with you.

DAN Now, that's enough of that. You come with me. (*To* JOSEPH *and* MARY.) We'll leave you on your own for a little, while we go and see to the flock, and then we'll all have a grand farewell supper. How's that, eh?

ELI That's a real good idea. We shan't be long.

(DAN, ELI *and* BOY *go off*.)

JOSEPH How kind they are. Do you think we ought to offer them money?

MARY Oh no. They would be most offended.

JOSEPH I suppose so. In any case we couldn't. I haven't got a penny left.

MARY Joseph! How are we going to get home?

JOSEPH The Lord will provide.

MARY Just as he provided the turtle-doves last week. I shall never forget the Temple, and that wonderful old man.

JOSEPH Old Simeon.

MARY I remember every word he said: Mine eyes have seen thy salvation—— A light to lighten the gentiles——

JOSEPH And the glory of thy people Israel.

MARY Yes, Joseph, the Lord will provide. I know that now, for this light can never be put out.

(*Enter* DAN.)

DAN Joseph, Mary, you have visitors.

MARY Oh, it's Elisabeth at last.

DAN No; three men on camels.

JOSEPH On camels?

DAN Great men by the look of them—and gentiles

JOSEPH Asking for us?

DAN Asking for the child. They say they have followed his star. They bring gifts.

MARY The Lord has provided. Let them come in, friend.

(DAN *goes off*.)

JOSEPH What does this mean?

MARY Gentiles shall come to thy light, and kings—Joseph, are they kings?

JOSEPH (*looking off*) They are very richly dressed. (*Indicating baby.*) Is he asleep?

MARY He has just opened his eyes.

JOSEPH Come and sit here.

(*Enter* CASPAR, MELCHIOR *and* BALTHASAR.)

CASPAR There is no doubt at all. This is the place, and yonder is the King. (*Kneeling.*) Lady, will you allow three strangers, not of your race, to pay our homage to your royal son? I bring a gift of gold. I pray that he may accept it.

MELCHIOR (*kneeling*) In my country, the highest worship we can offer is through frankincense. This gift I offer to the new-born King.

BALTHASAR (*kneeling*) My country is poor, but it produces one most valuable ointment called myrrh. This precious gift I beg him to receive.

MARY My lords, you are most kind. My son will be grateful. May I ask how you found your way here?

CASPAR By the stars, and with the help of the old King.

MARY The old King?

MELCHIOR He who lives in Jerusalem. What was his name?

BALTHASAR King Herod.

JOSEPH Herod!

CASPAR Come brothers, our task is done. We must take our leave and return. May fortune attend you.

MELCHIOR God's blessing be upon you.

BALTHASAR May peace be with you.

CASPAR We take the road.

(CASPAR, MELCHIOR *and* BALTHASAR *retire.*)

MARY Herod knows.

JOSEPH This is a trick. He is planning some evil. When they go back——

GABRIEL They go not back to Herod, for I say
They shall this day
Return to their own land another way.

MARY The Lord will provide.

JOSEPH But it won't be safe to travel north tomorrow, and we can't stay here.

GABRIEL Take up the child and Mary, as they stand;
Leave the shepherd band,
And flee for refuge into Egypt's land.

JOSEPH We must go south.

MARY To the desert?

JOSEPH To Egypt. It won't be the first time a Joseph has gone down into Egypt.

MARY And there to await an Exodus, when Pharaoh is dead.

JOSEPH When Herod is dead.

MARY It is written: Out of Egypt have I called my son.

JOSEPH Mary, I am so sorry——

MARY It is predestined.

JOSEPH I believe it is.

(*Enter* DAN, ELI *and* BOY.)

ELI Lord, what a marvel! Such camels! Such riches!

DAN What does it mean, Joseph?

JOSEPH It means that we must leave at once.

DAN You'll wait until the morning?

JOSEPH No, no, at once. There's not a moment to lose. Herod's soldiers will come here looking for us. Tell them nothing.

DAN Of course not.

ELI Not a word.

BOY I'll keep my mouth tight shut.

JOSEPH Good boy. Farewell, my good, kind friends. We shall meet again.

MARY I thank you, and my son thanks you too. God be with you.

DAN And with you. Farewell.

ELI Farewell.

BOY God be with you.

(JOSEPH *puts the gifts into his bundle.* MARY *and* JOSEPH *walk out, preferably down the centre through the audience, occasionally looking back to wave to the shepherds. Light fades from* DAN, ELI *and* BOY, *or they go off another way.*

During the final speech from the CHORUS, *all light disappears except the spotlight on the cross.*)

CHORUS   The light shines on in darkness,
          Uncomprehending darkness.
          Forces of Herod are strong,
          Evil and wrong.
          On they go in the darkness,
          Black Egyptian darkness,

Darkness that may be felt.
Hearts will melt
When Herod destroys
Bethlehem's boys.
The light shines on in darkness.
Such a frail spark
Alone in the dark,
Barely alive.
Can he survive?
Doesn't God care?
But isn't God there?
Now in our darkness
Still burns the flame;
He is the same
Then and today,
For ever and aye.
Why do we fear?
Isn't God here?
Even though torn
With scourge and with thorn,
Though hell assails
With spear and with nails,
Yet he will save
Through cross and grave,
Ending the night
In burning bright;
Dawn on our darkness,
Eternal Light!

CURTAIN